See the Difference with LearningCurve

LearningCurve
macmillan learning

learningcurveworks.com

LearningCurve is a winning solution for everyone: students come to class better prepared and instructors have more flexibility to go beyond the basic facts and concepts in class. LearningCurve's game-like quizzes are book-specific and link back to the textbook in LaunchPad so that students can brush up on the reading when they get stumped by a question. The reporting features help instructors track overall class trends and spot topics that are giving students trouble so that they can adjust lectures and class activities.

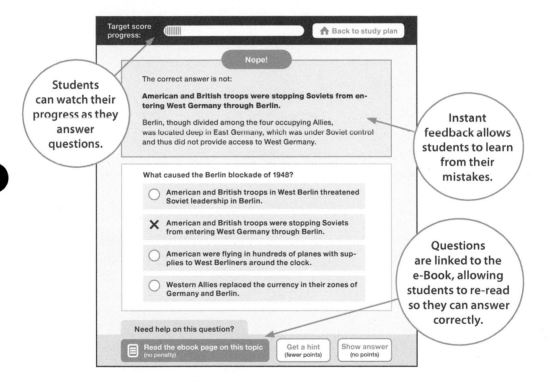

Students can watch their progress as they answer questions.

Instant feedback allows students to learn from their mistakes.

Questions are linked to the e-Book, allowing students to re-read so they can answer correctly.

LearningCurve is easy to assign, easy to customize, and easy to complete. See the difference LearningCurve makes in teaching and learning history.